My Little Golden Book About
Chicago

By Toyo Tyler
Illustrated by Barbara Bongini

A GOLDEN BOOK • NEW YORK

Text copyright © 2021 by Penguin Random House LLC. Cover and interior illustrations copyright © 2021 by Barbara Bongini. All righ̶ ̶ ̶ ̶ ̶ ̶ ̶ ̶ ̶ ̶ by Golden Books, an imprint of Random ̶ ̶ ̶ ̶ ̶ Penguin Random House LLC, 1745 Broadw̶ ̶ ̶ ̶ A Golden Book, A Little Golden Book, the G̶ ̶ ̶ ̶ ̶ are registered trademarks of F̶ ̶ ̶ ̶ ̶ rhcbook̶ Educators and librarians, for a variety of teachi̶ _̶ Library of Congress Control Number: 2020945413
ISBN 978-0-593-30449-5 (trade) — ISBN 978-0-593-30450-1 (ebook)
Printed in the United States of America
10 9 8 7 6 5 4 3 2 1

LINCOLN PARK ZOO

Hello! My name is Rory the Red Fox, and I live in **Chicago**, Illinois, which is also known as the Windy City. It's a beautiful day for some sightseeing. Would you like to join me?

Our first stop is the **Lincoln Park Zoo**, home to many different animals, including meerkats, two-toed sloths, and even adorable bear cubs.

Speaking of cubs, I know where
we should go next. . . .

Wrigley Field is another place to see cubs—
the Chicago Cubs baseball team, that is!

In addition to the ivy-covered brick outfield wall, Wrigley Field is famous for the old-fashioned, hand-turned scoreboard that sits atop the center-field bleachers. This baseball diamond is truly a jewel. Go, Cubs!

Chicago isn't just a baseball fan's paradise. It's a shopper's paradise, too! Let's take a stroll down the **Magnificent Mile**—a thirteen-block stretch of Michigan Avenue that features impressive skyscrapers, luxury hotels, and the world's finest stores.

After a long walk, nothing feels better than relaxing on the beach. These deep blue waters belong to **Lake Michigan**—one of the five Great Lakes in North America. Did you know there are twenty-four beaches in Chicago? Not bad for a city in the middle of the country!

Let's head down the shoreline of Lake Michigan to explore the spectacular **Navy Pier**! There's so much to do here. We can . . .

go AROUND and AROUND and AROUND
the Centennial Wheel . . .

try a slice of
Chicago's famous
deep-dish pizza . . .

and take a
cruise along . . .

the **Chicago River**, which runs through the city and is over 150 miles long! See if you can spot egrets, bats, deer, otters, and my red fox cousins who live along the river!

In the heart of Chicago is **Millennium Park**.
People gather here to enjoy the gardens,
outdoor art galleries, and live concerts.

Before you leave, don't forget to take a selfie
at **Cloud's Gate**—the gigantic silver sculpture
that is also known as the Bean!

Right next to Millennium Park is the **Art Institute of Chicago**. With more than 300,000 works of art, it is the second-largest art museum in the United States.

The lion sculptures that stand at the entrance weigh more than two tons each!

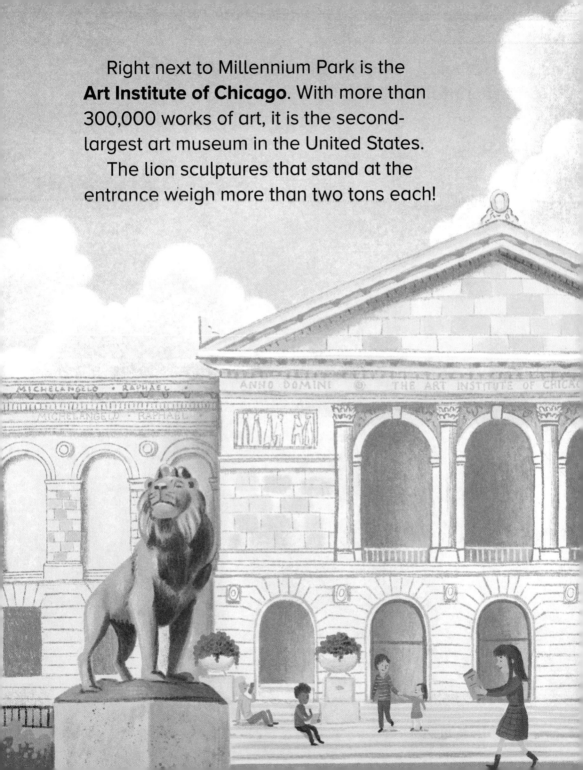

Our next stop is the impressive **Buckingham Fountain** in Grant Park. See those seahorses spouting water? There are four sets of them, and each set represents one of the states that borders Lake Michigan: Illinois, Wisconsin, Michigan, and Indiana.

Want to meet one of my good pals? This is Bella the Beluga Whale. Say hi, Bella! She's one of eight beluga whales (and one of 32,000 animals) who live here at **Shedd Aquarium**.

Just a few steps from the aquarium is the
Field Museum. Here you can learn about
ancient cultures and scientific discoveries.
You can also meet Máximo the Titanosaur,
the largest dinosaur to ever walk the earth.

And don't forget to visit SUE, the most complete T. rex skeleton ever discovered!

Here we are at **Adler Planetarium**—the first planetarium built in the United States. You can see amazing shows about the universe in the theater and look at celestial objects *trillions* of miles away through the giant telescope!

Welcome to **Willis Tower** (formerly known as the Sears Tower). It's the third-tallest building in the United States and one of the most popular attractions in Chicago. Are you ready to climb 110 stories to the very top?

Just kidding! We'll take the elevator.

If you're afraid of heights, this might not be the place for you. But if you're brave enough to step out onto this glass ledge, you'll be rewarded with a breathtaking view of Chicago!

Phew! It's so nice to be back on the ground. Our last stop of the day is the historic **Chicago Union Station**. Built more than ninety-five years ago, this train station is still one of the country's busiest.

More than 300 trains run through it every day.

Well, this is *my* train! I'm off to my next adventure.

Thank you for joining me on my walk through the Windy City. I hope it blew you away!